Fiona Macdonald

W
FRANKLIN WATTS
LONDON•SYDNEY

This edition 2011

First published in 2009 by
Franklin Watts
338 Euston Road
London NW1 3BH

Franklin Watts Australia
Level 17/207 Kent Street
Sydney NSW 2000

Copyright © Franklin Watts 2009

A CIP catalogue record for this book is
available from the British Library.

ISBN 978 1 4451 0616 8

Dewey classification: 940.53

Printed in China

Franklin Watts is a division of Hachette
Children's Books, an Hachette UK company.

www.hachette.co.uk

Series editor: Jeremy Smith
Art director: Jonathan Hair
Design: Jane Hawkins
Cover design: Jane Hawkins
Picture research: Diana Morris

Picture credits: Alamber/Shutterstock: 29.
AP/Topham: 14cr, The Art Archive: front cover
tr. Bettmann/Corbis: 18cr. Central Press/Hulton
Archive/Getty Images: 8tr, 12bl. Dorling
Kindersley/Getty Images: front cover tl.
Alfred Einstadt/Getty Images: 8bl. Fox
Photos/Getty Images: 10cr. Hulton
Archive/Getty Images: 16cr. Hulton-Deutsch
Collection/Corbis: front cover b, 16bl.
Hugo Jaeger/Time Life/Getty Images: 4.
Keystone/Getty Images: 1, 22bl. Bob
Landry/Time Life/Getty Images: 27. The
Lordprice Collection /Alamy: 20bl. The
Lordprice Collection/HIP/Topfoto: front cover
tc, 17, 23bc, 23br. MARKA/Alamy: 9.
Alfred Palmer/Time Life/Getty Images: 18bl.
Photos 12/Alamy: 24bl. Picturepoint/Topham:
13, 19, 24cr, 25, 26cr. Popperfoto/Getty Images:
11, 20cr, 26bl. Reg Speller/Hulton Archive/Getty
Images: 22cr. Topfoto: 12cr, 14bl, 15, 21.
Ullsteinbild/Topfoto: 5, 7.

Note to parents and teachers: Every effort has been made
by the Publishers to ensure that the websites detailed at
the back of this book are suitable for children, that they
are of the highest educational value, and that they contain
no inappropriate or offensive material. However, because
of the nature of the Internet, it is impossible to guarantee
that the contents of these sites will not be altered. We
strongly advise that Internet access is supervised by a
responsible adult.

Contents

World at War

For six terrible years, from 1939 to 1945, war raged around the world. It caused more death and destruction than any previous war, and still has an influence on our lives today. Historians call this conflict World War II.

Who fought?

World War II was fought between two groups of nations: the Allies (led by Britain and France) against the Axis powers (Germany, Italy, Japan and countries supporting them). The USSR (now Russia and nearby states) initially helped the Axis, but changed sides to join the Allies in 1941. The same year, the USA also joined in on the Allies' side.

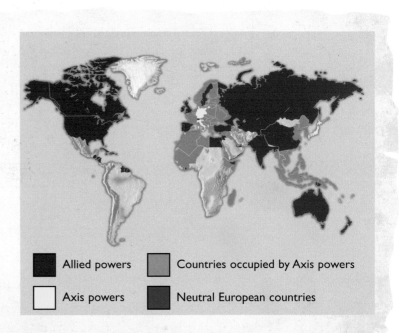

■ Allied powers		■ Countries occupied by Axis powers
□ Axis powers		■ Neutral European countries

Why war?

World War II began after Britain and France responded to Germany's invasion of Poland. Since 1933, Germany had been ruled by the extreme Nazi (National Socialist) Party, led by Adolf Hitler. The Nazis believed that Germans were the 'master race'. They demanded obedience.

◀ German leader Adolf Hitler salutes soldiers at a Nazi rally.

Hitler's plans

Hitler had grand plans to rebuild Germany's wealth, strength and pride after an earlier, crushing, defeat in World War I (1914-1918). He boosted Germany's military power, made friends with dictators in Italy and Spain, and began to attack neighbouring lands. On 3rd September, 1939, Britain issued a stern demand: Hitler must remove his invading army from Poland. He refused; so Britain declared war. This was to have consequences for almost everyone the world over, including children.

▼ German soldiers march into Poland, 1939.

War casualties

No-one knows precisely how many people died during World War II. But historians have made the following estimates, based on government records:

• Soldiers, sailors, aircrew - around 20 million (about one in five of all who fought)

• Civilians - around 25 million, worldwide

This was the largest loss of life in war that the world had ever seen. Around half of the civilian victims were children.

Nazi Germany

Hitler hoped that a strong, united Nazi Germany could rule the world. He made plans to 'purify' all German-controlled lands by getting rid of his political enemies and some ethnic minority groups, such as Jews and gypsies.

Terror tactics

Nazi racial theories taught that Jews in particular were to be despised. They blamed them for all that was wrong in Europe, and taught that a Jew could never be a German. In 1933, books by Jewish writers were burned. In 1935, Hitler's government took citizenship rights away from all Jews. Many Jews lost their jobs. Jewish children were banned from schools. Some families escaped, mostly to Britain or the USA, or managed to smuggle their children abroad. But many Jews were trapped in German lands - penniless and in danger. In November 1938, on 'Kristallnacht' (Night of Broken Glass), Nazi mobs smashed Jewish homes and businesses, terrorising parents and children.

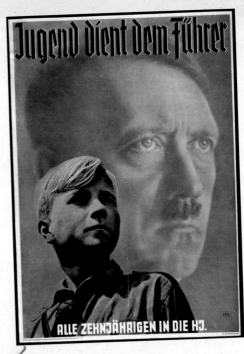

▲ This poster encouraged German young people to follow Hitler.

◀ Jewish adults and children in Nazi Germany were forced to wear yellow badges, to show that they were 'second-class citizens'.

Hitler Youth

Before and during the war, Hitler forced all other non-Jewish families to support his plans. Even children had to join 'Hitler Youth' groups. From the age of ten, they were trained to be tough and strong. They went for mountain hikes, and practised gym and athletics. Boys learned to handle weapons, and girls were taught to care for 'children, the Church and the kitchen'.

Kristallnacht

" ... at about 3 o'clock in the morning, there was an insistent ringing on the bell. When I went to the main door, I heard several male voices cursing and yelling to us to open up at once. This was like a raid by burglars; we immediately ran onto one of our balconies and shouted for help. Then we discovered that a group of men had got into the garden, and they shouted at us to be quiet at once or they would shoot. Then we realised that it was a Nazi attack."

A Jewish child in Nazi Germany remembers the terror of Kristallnacht.

Children's clothes

Young people were encouraged to wear German national costume (shorts, boots, tight jackets and felt hats for boys; white, puff-sleeved blouses under dresses with full skirts, close-fitting bodices and decorative aprons for girls.) They learned traditional German country dances and rousing, patriotic songs. Tall, blonde children (Hitler thought that these were 'ideal Germans') were kidnapped from their parents and given to top Nazis to raise, as future leaders of Germany.

▶ This page from a Hitler Youth booklet shows a smiling girl with her hair in a traditional style.

Alle 10jährigen zu uns

Divided Families

On both sides of the fighting, the war divided families. Separated husbands and wives, brothers and sisters, parents and children all learned to live with fear and sorrow and prayed for the end of the war.

Marriage

Because wartime life was so uncertain, many young couples got married in a hurry, before the bridegroom was 'called up' to fight. They were keen to have 'wartime babies', as a symbol of faith in a better future. But all healthy young men had to leave home to fight, and so many children grew up hardly knowing their fathers. Millions of men were killed in battle, never having seen their new-born sons or daughters.

▲ Mothers and babies wave goodbye as young men march off to war.

Orphans

Many families were divided when their homes were destroyed. By the end of the war in 1945, there were around 100 million refugees worldwide. Many were orphaned children, whose parents had been killed. Other children had been parted from their families during the fighting; they lived wild amid ruined buildings, or were cared for by strangers.

▲ A father in uniform says goodbye to his new baby.

Waiting for news

Living apart was miserable, especially when there was no news of loved ones. Wartime letters might take weeks to arrive, or be lost altogether. Telephone calls across enemy territory were almost impossible. Telegrams meant bad news: a family member had died, or was 'missing in action'. These messages were often delivered by boys as young as 14 years old.

▶ A soldier at an army camp in Italy posts a letter home.

Songs of the war

Lines from popular World War II songs. They are all about parting:

'Wish me luck as you wave me goodbye!'

'We'll meet again, don't know where, don't know when ...'

'I'll be seeing you in all the old familiar [usual] places ...'

The Home Front

World War II was a new type of war. For the first time, ordinary, peaceful civilians - men, women and children - became the main targets of attack. Planes bombed houses, schools and hospitals. Quiet streets became war zones.

Taking shelter

In Britain, some families built metal bomb shelters in their gardens, and 'refuge rooms' in cellars. Children helped to fill these with emergency supplies: blankets, torches and batteries, bottles of water, tinned food, disinfectant, bandages. They also helped to put up 'black-out' curtains to stop the light from house windows guiding enemy bombers at night. They filled rows of buckets with water, ready to extinguish fires.

▲ A child sleeps on a hammock in an air-raid shelter that has been decorated for Christmas.

▲ A wartime gas mask (right), seen from the front. It was carried in the box on the left.

Gas masks

Adults and children made sure that they always carried their gas masks with them, in case of a poison-gas attack. By 1939, 44 million masks had been handed out by the government in Britain alone! British children's gas masks were specially designed to look like favourite cartoon character Mickey Mouse - but they were hot and stuffy to wear, and smelled horrible.

Teen helpers

Older children helped to dig ditches or build barricades to stop advancing armies. They ran through dark, bombed streets with urgent messages for firefighters and air-raid wardens. Some teenage boys lied about their age to join volunteer troops of defenders, such as the British 'Home Guard'.

▶ Children help to fill bags with sand to build a protective wall against bombs.

Stirring speeches

Children – and adults – were inspired to defend the Home Front by stirring speeches from Britain's wartime leader, Winston Churchill:

'We shall defend our island whatever the cost may be. We shall fight on the beaches, we shall fight on the landing grounds, we shall fight in the fields and in the streets... we shall never surrender!'

Sent to Safety

Wartime cities and towns were very dangerous places. Streets were lined with collapsing buildings and littered with broken glass. Fire bombs and landmines dropped by planes might explode at any time.

Evacuation

City parents in many lands sent their children away to live in safety with friends or relatives in the countryside, or even overseas. In Britain, the government organised mass transportation of city children to country homes in 1939. This was known as 'Evacuation'.

▲ Railway staff escort a group of evacuees to a train.

Saying goodbye

Mothers were told to pack a small bag for each child, with essentials such as soap, a toothbrush, nightwear and a favourite toy. They then had to take children to a government rallying point: a local school, or a railway station. There, workers tied a label to each child, stating his or her name and destination. They led groups of children on board special trains, while mothers waved goodbye, fighting back their tears.

▲ Child evacuees cuddle their favourite toys and holding cardboard boxes containing their gas masks.

Evacuation tragedy

For extra safety, some British parents chose to send their children to friendly nations far away, such as Australia, South Africa and the USA. The children travelled by sea; cheap passenger aircraft had not yet been invented. But in 1940, a British passenger liner, the SS *Benares*, was sunk by a German submarine as it sailed across the Atlantic Ocean, heading for Canada. There were 90 British children on board; only 11 survived.

New homes

At the end of the journey, volunteer helpers took children to meet their foster parents. All evacuated children found their new homes strange at first. Many had never been to the countryside, or seen crops growing in fields, or met farm animals. Some children settled happily; for them, evacuation was an exciting adventure. But others were homesick or very miserable, especially if their foster families were mean, thoughtless or cruel.

▶ A volunteer leads a girl evacuee to her new home in a country cottage.

In the Blitz

Not all boys and girls spent the war safely in the countryside. Back in big cities, children and adults faced the chance of death every night: no-one knew when the next air raid would be.

Blitzkrieg (the Blitz)

In World War II, new technology was used by both sides to attack from the air. Mass bombing raids on civilians started with the German 'Blitzkrieg' (Lightning War, 1940-1941) when German planes dropped bombs on British cities almost every night. These included thousands of firebombs, which caused massive death and destruction. They were followed by 'doodlebugs' (unmanned flying bombs) and powerful rockets in 1944 and 1945.

▲ The city of Hiroshima, Japan, was flattened by the world's first atom bomb.

Allied fightback

The Allies soon fought back. British bombs killed more than 130,000 people in one night at Dresden, an historic city in Germany. In 1945, US bombers dropped the most deadly weapons of all - newly-invented atom bombs - on the Japanese cities of Hiroshima and Nagasaki. Up to 140,000 died at Hiroshima after the bombing and 80,000 in Nagasaki.

▲ Stunned families stagger through the ruins of their houses after a bomb attack on Coventry, England.

Black-out!

During air raids, children and parents huddled together in shelters, or stumbled through the blacked-out streets to hide in underground railway stations. These were crowded, hot, noisy and frightening. Few children managed to sleep peacefully there. Once the 'all clear' siren sounded, it was safe to leave - and find out whether houses and streets were still standing. Families made homeless by bombing raids boarded in hostels run by volunteers, or stayed with friends.

▼ Hungry children crowd round a food stall run by women volunteers.

SIFTING THE EVIDENCE

Remembering the Blitz

'... that day stands out like a flaming wound in my memory. Imagine a ground-floor flat crowded with hysterical women, crying babies and great crashes in the sky and the whole earth shaking. Someone rushed in: "The docks are alight. All the docks are alight." I could smell burning...

Everything was chaos, except for the fire which was like a living monster ... I could see my mother standing there screaming for her children... "They're coming tonight. Quick! Quick!"

Bernad Kops, a London child, remembers the Blitz.

(Source: Juliet Gardiner, War Children*)*

15

War Effort

Food, drink, clothes, fuel, medicines and raw materials for industry were all in short supply during the war. Rationing was introduced (see pages 18-19). Governments urged civilians to make a special 'war effort', and find new ways of surviving.

Helping out

Children did their best. They grew vegetables to eat, kept pigs, rabbits and chickens for meat and eggs, and gathered wild foods, such as mushrooms and nettles. They learned how to mend old clothes and toys or make new ones from scraps. In cities, they set up clubs to collect rubbish and scrap metal. Bones and cooking fat were collected and used to make explosives.

▲ Boys from a school in south-east England go to the fields to help pick rhubarb.

Pocket money pledge

Schools and youth groups raised money to help pay for new ships and planes. Children also helped the war effort by putting their pocket money in government savings schemes. That way, the government could borrow it to pay for troops and weapons.

◀ A young girl counts the pennies she has collected for deposit in her savings bank, as her contribution to the war effort.

Women at work

The war effort changed the way people worked. For the first time, women laboured in factories. They drove trains, buses and ambulances, delivered mail, ploughed fields, worked on farms and ran government offices. By doing work that was usually reserved for men, they freed male staff to fight. But they had little spare time for their families. After school, many children were cared for in government-run nurseries, or by grandparents and neighbours. In some countries, such as the USSR, children as young as ten worked in factories, alongside women.

▶ Women working in a munitions factory fill shells with explosives.

WORLD WAR II LEGACY

Towards equality

Wartime mothers proved that they could succeed in many jobs, and make sure that their children were well looked after. Their strength, bravery and determination won great praise – and inspired many women to seek careers after the war. But they found that peacetime employers preferred to recruit men. So women protested. Years later, in the 1970s and 1980s, governments passed laws giving equal working rights to women and men.

Fair Shares

Farming and food production were severely disrupted by the war. To stop people starving, governments introduced rationing. They limited the amount of food that anyone, rich or poor, could buy, to provide fair shares for all.

Rationing

Each man, woman, child - and baby - was given his or her own ration book. It listed how much rationed food they were allowed each week, and recorded their purchases. New laws also made wasting food a crime; one London chef was fined for letting mice eat scraps in his restaurant kitchen.

▲ Children queue up for milk in a British primary school.

Small portions

Rationed items included many nourishing and tasty foods: meat, fish, cheese, eggs, milk, butter, beans, sugar, tea, jam, tinned fruit, cakes, biscuits, cooking fat and chocolate. Ration portions were very small. For example, British adults were allowed just 84g of cheese, 1.7 litres milk, and one egg per week! Children were allowed extra milk plus bottled orange juice, to help them grow tall and strong.

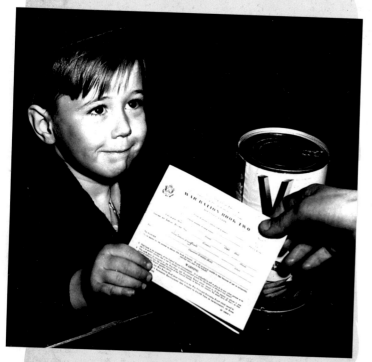

▲ A child hands a shopkeeper his ration book.

Wartime starvation

On mainland Europe and in Asia, food shortages were very severe. In Russian cities surrounded by German armies, starving families ate dogs, cats, rats and even dead bodies. Wartime famines in China and the Indian sub-continent killed millions of people, including babies and children.

Good food habits

Although wartime meals were plain and simple, rations in Britain and the USA provided a well-balanced diet. People became much healthier, and, as you can see from the photos in this book, almost everyone was very slim. The children and young people who survived World War II have lived much longer than earlier generations, partly because of their healthy wartime rations. Many are still alive today, over 60 years after the war.

▶ A week's worth of rationed foods. Bread, potatoes, green vegetables and wild foods were not rationed.

Make Do and Mend

In most nations, everyday items were rationed, alongside food. Many raw materials - cotton, sheeps' wool, rubber and leather - could not be imported easily. If supplies did arrive, they were used to make uniforms and boots for the troops.

No frills

Many young men spent the war in uniform. Clothes for women, boys and girls also copied army styles, with belted waists and square shoulders. By law, they had to use as little fabric as possible, so skirts were short and straight. In Britain, frills on girls' and womens' underwear were banned, because they were wasteful. Most boys wore shorts - even at school - until their mid-teens.

▲ This female car mechanic is doing a typically male job, and wearing men's clothes – trousers.

Women in trousers

For the first time, it became acceptable for women and girls to wear trousers. They were warm and practical for wartime work. A feminine version of army battle-dress, called a 'siren suit', was high fashion for young women. Also popular were home-made hats, sewn from scraps of warm woollen cloth in an amazing range of styles.

▲ Wartime fashions for young women.

Repair and re-wear

Everyone was encouraged to 'make do and mend'. This meant repairing and re-using old clothes and shoes, rather than buying new ones. Girls and boys were taught how to replace buttons, patch torn clothes and darn holes in socks - and how to knit warm woolly scarves and gloves to send to troops fighting overseas. Girls also learned to make new frocks by stitching together scraps from old clothes. Stripy knitwear, made from wool recycled from worn-out jumpers, was very popular.

▶ These children are being fitted with second-hand shoes.

From UK Government pamphlet:
LONGER LIFE FOR LINEN!

- To renovate worn sheets:
  Double sheets, cut out the thin part, put sides to middle, sew neatly. Single sheets put patch on wrong side.

- Worn-out towels. Take two towels and quilt them together.

- Hand towels from bath towels. Cut them from the good parts of worn big towels.

Childhood Fun – and Fighting

Parents tried to make sure that children had as much fun as possible. Even at playtime, however, children could not forget the fighting. The most popular toys and games all had a war theme.

Toys

Children played with toy soldiers and guns. Board games and jigsaws featured planes, warships and flags. There was no TV in wartime, but governments broadcast special children's programmes on the radio. At the cinema, everyone watched the news, cartoons, war adventures, and comedies mocking Hitler. Best-selling authors wrote wartime stories about favourite children's characters, such as 'Just William'.

▶ Father and son – both in airforce uniform – play with a splendid toy plane.

Bombsites

Children enjoyed exploring bombsites (this was very dangerous) and collecting war 'treasures', such as pieces of shrapnel. They played noisy battle games. But many were also keen to join in real fighting. Some were fiercely proud of their country and wanted to defend it. Others were angry and disturbed by the horrors they had seen. They wanted revenge.

◀ Dangerous – but exciting! Young boys play on a bombsite.

Movies

Many wartime movies remained popular for years after the war, and are still sometimes screened today on TV. How many of these have you seen or heard of?

- 1939 *The Lion Has Wings* (UK) Air Force recruitment
- 1940 *The Great Dictator* (USA) Comedy mocking Hitler
- 1941 *Dangerous Moonlight* (UK) Battle of Britain
- 1942 *Casablanca* (USA) Romance and Spies
- 1942 *One of Our Aircraft is Missing* (UK) On the Run in Enemy Territory
- 1943 *In Which We Serve* (UK) Navy heroes

Youth organisations

Boys and girls enrolled in youth organisations such as the Scouts, Guides and (in the USA) Junior Commando teams. They learned how to recognise approaching enemy aircraft, how to send messages using semaphore (flag signals) or morse code, and emergency first aid. In Nazi-occupied Europe, children joined secret resistance groups, risking their lives to act as lookouts, carry messages, take food to Jewish people in hiding, and help Allied troops escape. In Russia and Germany, boys as young as 12 joined the army and fought with real guns.

▼ These playing cards helped children learn to recognise enemy aircraft (below left) and allied aircraft (below right).

J is for **JUNKERS** *our enemy of course*

H is for **HURRICANE** *never known to fail*

The Holocaust

In 1941, Nazi leader Adolf Hitler made careful plans for mass murder. He called them the 'Final Solution' to all Germany's problems. All Jews and other 'undesirable' groups would be sent to extermination camps where most would die.

In the ghetto

Before being sent to extermination camps, many Jewish families were rounded up and crammed into old prisons, or locked inside crowded city districts called 'ghettoes'. Conditions there were grim. But parents bravely tried to make life for their children as normal as possible, as did kindly Jewish volunteers, who cared for orphaned Jewish children. They ran schools, organised games, told stories, played music, held concerts and celebrated traditional Jewish festivals.

▶ Jewish girls stand beside the ghetto wall that keeps them prisoner in their own home city.

▲ The wartime diaries written by Jewish teenager Anne Frank (see box, opposite) still survive today.

Hiding away

Some Jewish parents and children tried to escape Hitler's Final Solution by going into hiding. They built secret shelters, tucked away in big old buildings, and relied on brave, loyal friends to bring them food and water. But most were discovered - or betrayed - and captured.

Two teenage heroes

The diary kept by Jewish schoolgirl Anne Frank reveals how terrifying - and frustrating - hiding from the Nazis could be. With her family, she spent two dreadful years shut away in secret rooms, in the Netherlands. Tragically, the Franks were betrayed and sent to a concentration camp, where Anne died aged 16.

Young Jewish student Mordecai Anielewicz led a rebellion in the ghetto at Warsaw, Poland's capital city. He wanted to stop the Nazis from sending the Polish Jews to concentration camps. Although Mordecai and his friends were outnumbered by German soldiers, they battled bravely for weeks. Mordecai died fighting.

Extermination camps

Captured Jews were herded onto cattle wagons, like animals, and taken to concentration camps. There, it was hell on earth. Men, women and children were worked to death, gassed or poisoned. Some were tortured first. Around six million Jews died, together with gypsies, political prisoners and other groups that Hitler deemed undesirable.

▶ Jewish children gather in a Nazi camp. Can you see the high barbed wire fences?

After the War

In 1945, when World War II ended, men, women and children were delighted. At last, they could look forward to a peaceful future, instead of one filled with hatred and fear.

The end of the war

To begin with, in many lands, there was singing and dancing. But once the parties were over, people realised just how weak and tired they were after five long years of fighting. They had lost family members, neighbours, workmates and schoolfriends. Their homes and cities had been destroyed. They had no work, no food and no money; many were homeless.

▼ Celebrating victory with a street party in 1945.

▲ Relieved and very happy, a family crowds round a fighting man who has returned home safely.

Changed forever

Millions of women were widows; millions more children were orphans. They all faced peacetime alone and grieving. Even happy, reunited, families found it difficult to settle down to 'normal' life again. Children had missed years of schooling, or been mentally scarred by bombing raids. Many families were homeless; parents and children crowded into grandparents' houses, or shared apartments with strangers.

Working for peace

The USA sent generous aid - known as the 'Marshall Plan' to rebuild war-torn Europe and Japan. Even so, food, clothes and fuel were still rationed, for years. But governments - and parents - were determined to make a new and better world for their children. They designed new towns, set up new businesses, and built new schools, parks and playgrounds. In Britain, a new 'Welfare State' was created, to care for citizens 'from the cradle to the grave'.

▶ Elected in 1945 at the end of the war, Prime Minister Clement Attlee (1883-1951) set up Britain's first Welfare State.

WORLD WAR II LEGACY

Building for the future

Some wartime survivors felt guilty. They were still alive, but so many millions had died. The Holocaust (see page 24-25) had challenged their religious beliefs, and their faith in humanity. Many survivors felt that they must try to prevent another world war. In 1945, they founded the United Nations organisation (UN), to work for world peace. In 1957, former enemies Germany and France joined together in friendship with other nations in Europe to set up a 'Common Market' (now the European Union).

Activities

Even in wartime, children found ways of having fun. Helped by parents or teachers, they made their own toys and learned to cook plain but nourishing wartime foods.

Make a Scrap Glove-Puppet

You will need:

• an old sock - large, thick and clean!

• scraps of old cloth

• fabric glue OR a needle and thread

• lengths of wool, string or old ribbon

• scissors

• pen and paper (optional)

1. Decide what kind of animal your puppet will be. Draw a design if you like.

2. Cut out its nose, ears and eyes from the cloth scraps. Stick or sew them on to the closed end of the sock.

3. Using cloth, ribbon or string, cut out and sew or stick on hair, whiskers or a mane. You could add cloth fangs, and a tongue, and spikes or scales as well, if you like.

4. Put your hand inside the sock and wiggle your fingers to make your puppet 'come alive'.

Matching flags game

In wartime, children were trained to recognise flags and uniforms from friendly and enemy nations, and to report anything suspicious that they saw to the police, air raid wardens or teachers.

You will need:

• a book or website with pictures of national flags from the following nations: Germany, Italy, Japan, Britain, France, USA. Each nation played an important part in World War II.

• a packet of plain postcards (approx 48 cards).

• a ruler, pencil, felt-tips or crayons.

• a friend to help make drawings and to play the game with.

1. Look carefully at the flag pictures.

2. Copy each flag on to a separate postcard and colour it in.

3. Repeat your drawings, three times more for each flag. If possible, get a friend to help you with this. You should end up with 48 cards.

4. Shuffle the cards, and deal them to two, three or four players. Play the game like 'Snap'.

Lord Woolton pie

This was named after a well-known government minister in charge of wartime food supplies. Ask an adult to help you with this cooking.

You will need:

- about 500g (total, scrubbed, peeled weight) of any solid vegetables, for example: potatoes, swedes, cauliflower and carrots

- a small onion or a few spring onions

- a teaspoonful (10 ml) of yeast extract (eg Marmite or similar)

- a tablespoonful (20 ml) of oatmeal

- about 400 ml hot water

- wholemeal, low-fat pastry OR mashed potato to cover

Method:

1. Scrub, peel and chop the vegetables neatly. Put them in a pan with the water, yeast extract and oatmeal. Stir gently over a low heat for ten minutes.

2. Pour the mixture into an ovenproof dish. Top with a thin layer of pastry or potato.

3. Bake at around 180°C for 20-30 minutes, until the pastry or potato topping is crisp and light brown.

4. Serve with gravy. In wartime, this might have been made by heating animal skin and bones until they were brown, adding water, then boiling them for a long time.

Wartime Breakfast Cereal – Porridge!

The energy (calories) in porridge is released very slowly. This stopped wartime people from feeling hungry for hours.

For each person, you will need:

- about 25g oatmeal

- about 200 ml cold water

Method:

1. Put the oatmeal and water in a small saucepan. Stir. Cover with a lid and leave overnight.

2. Next morning, remove the lid. Then heat the porridge gently until it boils, stirring all the time.

3. Turn the heat as low as possible, and leave the porridge to simmer for ten minutes, stirring occasionally.

4. If you like, sprinkle in a tiny pinch of salt when the porridge is cooked.

Today, when food is plentiful, you might like to add chopped fresh or dried fruit to your porridge. Yummy!

Timeline

1918 End of World War I. Germany is defeated.

1929 Start of the Great Depression (worldwide economic crisis).

1933 Adolf Hitler, leader of the German Nazi (National Socialist) party, becomes German Chancellor (leader).

1938 Kristallnacht (Night of Broken Glass): Nazis smash Jewish homes and businesses.

March 1938 Hitler takes over Austria and parts of Czechoslovakia

September 1938 Munich Agreement: Britain agrees to friendship with Hitler because it is not yet strong enough to go to war.

1 September, 1939 Hitler invades Poland.

3 September, 1939 Britain and France declare war on Germany.

May 1940 Hitler invades Belgium, the Netherlands and France.

June 1940 The 'Battle of Britain' takes place between the German air force and the British RAF.

1940- 1941 The Blitz takes place.

June 1941 Hitler invades Russia. Russia becomes ally of Britain and France.

December 1941 Japan (Hitler's ally) bombs US warships at Pearl Harbour, Hawaii. The USA joins the war as an ally of Britain and France.

February 1943 Hitler's army defeated at Battle of Stalingrad, Russia.

September 1943 Hitler's main European ally, Italy, surrenders.

6 June, 1944 'D-Day'. Allies invade Nazi-occupied Europe.

February 1945 Russians invade Germany, and start to free Jewish prisoners in concentration camps.

April 1945 Russians reach Berlin. Hitler kills himself and Germany surrenders

August 1945 US planes drop the world's first nuclear weapons on Japanese cities. Japan surrenders.

Glossary and further information

Allies Britain, France and nations that fought with them against Hitler, including the USA, the USSR, Canada, Australia, New Zealand and South Africa.

Axis Hitler's Germany, and the nations that fought on its side, including Italy and Japan.

civilians ordinary men, women and children who do not belong to the armed forces.

dictator a ruler who has absolute, unrestricted control over government.

evacuee someone who has been evacuated from their home, school or workplace.

ghetto crowded city district where minority groups, especially Jewish people, were forced to live.

Holocaust Nazi plan to exterminate some ethnic groups, particularly Jews.

Kristallnacht ('Night of Broken Glass') event in 1938 when Nazis smashed Jewish homes and businesses in Germany and Austria.

Nazi supporter of the extreme National Socialist party in Germany. The Nazis aimed to make Germany great. They passed many unjust laws and tried to exterminate all minority groups.

semaphore a way of sending signals using flags.

shrapnel sharp pieces of metal from broken weapons or exploded ammunition.

war crime a terrible action that breaks the normal rules of war, for example, killing defenceless civilians.

Finding out more about life during the war

There are museums and websites you can visit to find out more about children's lives during WWII.

www.bbc.co.uk/history/ww2children

An excellent interactive site about children in wartime.

www.bbc.co.uk/scotland/education/as/ww2/index.shtml

A website about Scotland in wartime.

www.woodlands-junior.kent.sch.uk/Homework/Britain.html

A website by teachers and children for other children with of information about World War II.

http://pinelake.bloomfield.org/mediacenter/ww2forkids.htm

A very helpful website that tells you how to use the Internet to find all kinds of information about World War II.

Index